A STEP-BY-STEP GUIDE TO STARTING AN EFFECTIVE MENTORING PROGRAM

Dr. Norman H. Cohen

HRD Press
Amherst, Massachusetts

Published by   HRD Press
                22 Amherst Road
                Amherst, MA 01001 USA
                1-800-822-2801 (U.S. and Canada)
                1-413-253-3488
                1-413-253-3490 (Fax)
                http://www.hrdpress.com

ISBN 0-87245-567-8
Production services by CompuDesign
Cover design by Eileen Klockars
Editorial services by Robie Grant

Printed in Canada

Contents

CONTENTS

CONTENTS

Introduction

◆

A Step-by-Step Guide to Starting an Effective Mentoring Program offers practical guidance to coordinators who are responsible for starting and operating a mentoring program *after* the decision has been made to introduce it.

The underlying assumption is that they will be best served by material that primarily focuses on application—planning, developing, and problem solving—rather than on exploring the theory or philosophy of mentoring for adult learners. There are already other works that fulfill this requirement (see Appendix).

In actual workplace situations, senior administrators will usually be responsible for appointing program managers (coordinators) as well as for authorizing the allocation of basic resources, such as funds and personnel. From this vantage point, this book is very beneficial for executives who need a *preliminary* overview of the expertise and budget required to establish, conduct, and maintain a properly organized and productive one-to-one model of learning in the workplace.

Thus exposed in the *early* stages of planning to the concept that mentoring is a *unique* method, decision makers considering this approach will be better able to:

1. determine the most suitable staff to introduce mentoring into their organization
2. support an interpersonal model that balances the achievement of individual employee (mentee) objectives with the fulfillment of organizational goals

Planners must understand the basic mentoring model of learning because a sponsored program must be *accurately conceptualized if it is to be applied correctly* in the workplace. If the program is constructed on a realistic foundation of tangible resources, the special opportunity offered by the one-to-one approach can be incorporated successfully into the daily behaviors of mentors and mentees.

ADULT PSYCHOLOGY BASIS

This *Guide* is based on the premise that coordinators possess specific knowledge and insight into the educational concept referred to as "mentoring" and understand how mentoring is different from other activities such as coaching and career counseling. Moreover, for the program to genuinely succeed as a legitimate enterprise, the coordinator must fully comprehend the complex dynamics of the mentor–mentee relationship as it develops within the context of the contemporary organization. Mentoring must be carefully planned, implemented in proper sequence, and shepherded through its pilot phases.

It is extremely important that coordinators are knowledgeable about mentoring because a central assumption underlying the interactive model is that a viable program must be based on recognized principles of adult psychology, with a special focus on developing the competency of mentor practitioners to apply the six interpersonal behaviors that ultimately blend to form the holistic mentoring model of one-to-one learning (see Appendix for suggested reading).

MENTOR AND MENTEE DEVELOPMENT

A key function of coordinators will be to operate programs that assist other professionals to function proficiently in the *role of mentor*. Effectively conducted mentoring projects, which include proper administrative support, focused training sessions, and appropriate group meetings, will enable mentors to actively promote career development that is relevant to the work-related skills and career growth of their mentees.

Furthermore, program managers need to ensure that employees in the *role of mentee* are properly oriented as well to their own responsibilities so they can constructively respond to the potential offered by involvement in mentoring. Coordinators must also be prepared to invest resources in the proper orientations and follow-up sessions necessary to develop the proficiencies of the mentees, not just of the mentors.

COMPLEMENTARY ROLES

A priority for the coordinator will be to clarify the expectations of their different but *complementary* roles to both mentors and mentees. It is important to explain the implications of dual responsibilities so that the commitment and tasks involved are fully understood at the beginning of the relationship.

In order for participants to recognize that they are entering into a workplace relationship that requires them to fulfill mutual obligations, the coordinator must clarify two related points at the center of the one-to-one learning experience:

+ *collaborative* interpersonal relations form the substantive core of mentor–mentee contact
+ *joint commitment* allows mentees and mentors to participate as partners who together construct a valuable interactive journey

UNIFIED SOURCE OF INFORMATION

Those planning a mentoring program must possess a coherent understanding rather than a fragmented view of its components. Such unified knowledge will help to ensure that a solid administrative foundation is created within the current organization, and thereby increase the probability that efficient, consistent, and meaningful one-to-one learning becomes the operational model in the workplace.

ORGANIZATION OF CONTENTS

A central objective of this book is to provide a descriptive map of the key decisions and actions required to create a logically constructed mentoring program. It is arranged into four major sections:

◆ Step One: Understanding the Coordinator's Responsibilities—Overall scope of project arranged in a sequence which highlights six specific components

◆ Step Two: Identifying Participants—Review of institutional priorities relevant to decisions about issues and procedures for identifying/selecting participants

◆ Step Three: Conducting the Matching Process—Pairing of mentors and mentees, especially issues related to preferences

◆ Step Four: Orientation and Training—Plans for orientation, training, and follow-up

The material also is designed to allow users to follow a step-by-step sequence of detailed guidelines. As an application model, this approach will allow coordinators to:

◆ grasp the *magnitude* of the complete project
◆ understand the separate *components* necessary to start an effective program
◆ identify the specific administrative *resources* required to create meaningful learning opportunities
◆ rely on practical *experience* instead of the assumptions posed by an idealized or untested model

SELF-CONTAINED APPROACH

A Step-to-Step Guide to Starting an Effective Mentoring Program has been designed to serve numerous purposes as a core administrative handbook. As a self-contained guide to creating a complete program, the book also provides access to a package of valid and reliable materials expressly created for use in new or already operational programs, such as a self-assessment inventory, a critique form for training, and books for both mentors and mentees (see Appendix).

REFERENCE TO OTHER MATERIAL

For those presently in the "learning about" rather than the recommendation stage, I suggest reviewing the works listed in the Appendix as part of their initial effort to acquire information about the field of adult mentoring.

The collection of books cited has been included primarily to provide a complete set of materials that can be used directly in the formation and management of an operational program. They can also serve as valuable references by offering preliminary guidance regarding the mentoring model of learning, with a particular focus on understanding:

- the *principles* of adult psychology underlying the mentoring relationship
- the fundamental *knowledge* required to successfully create a complete mentoring program

STEP ONE

Understanding the Coordinator's Responsibilities

◆

1.   RECOGNIZE THE IMPORTANCE OF POSITION

The appointment of the coordinator should be considered a message of executive support as well as a necessary operational decision if the mentoring program is to proceed as a credible project. The coordinator should be prepared to function as an official program representative at *all levels* of the organization.

COORDINATOR INFLUENCE

Five practical factors determine the success of the coordinator as a positive influence on the outcome of the project:

1. *access* to those who can authorize specific resources
2. *proficiency* in interpersonal and social skills
3. *capacity* to develop workable plans
4. *ability* to handle managerial details
5. *knowledge* of the organizational culture

A full-time manager may not always be necessary, especially if the pilot project involves a small group of participants. Often, the preliminary planning and early stages of development can be accomplished by someone who assumes half- or part-time accountability.

However, the individual who accepts responsibility for the position of coordinator must be sure that those delegating the task fully understand that the job will require appropriate dedication and *time* if the program is to be conducted effectively. Moreover, the eventual need for a full-time coordinator should also be considered as a realistic probability by all concerned *at the very beginning* to ensure that a quality operation is maintained as more employees (possibly at various levels) become active participants. The administrative demands on the coordinator should be expected to increase rather than to stabilize or decrease.

2.   CONSTRUCT A REALISTIC PLAN

To ensure that the members of the organization view the mentoring model as based on *realistic* planning, the coordinator of the program should formulate (and share) a detailed written explanation that describes how mentoring will be:

- *integrated* into the overall institutional mission
- *implemented* as a meaningful opportunity for employees to engage in workplace competency and skill acquisition
- *based* on clear operational guidelines and relevant training
- *utilized* by individual participants as a valuable career and professional development experience

DETERMINE THE SCOPE OF THE PROJECT

Although many mentoring programs start as modest endeavors, even at the pilot project stage it is important to consider the longer-range plan of development—at least two to three years ahead. Of course, the immediate focus will quite naturally be on the demands of launching a program in the present and not on some distant spot on the horizon.

IMMEDIATE PROGRAMMATIC CONCERNS

If the current plan, for example, is to initiate a limited program at a single entry point, and to recruit only mid-level managers to mentor junior technical or support staff for about twelve months, then the scope of responsibilities would involve dealing with five major concerns:

- ◆ *allocations*—funds and resources
- ◆ *appointments*—administrative staff
- ◆ *identifying, selecting, and matching participants*—mentors and mentees
- ◆ *orientation and training*—all participants (including a special session for supervisors of mentees)
- ◆ *management*—daily functioning of program

The third and fourth points should be viewed as of particular significance because of the relatively complex logistics required to recruit, select, match, orient, and train the participants.

Even a reasonably streamlined process will be relatively time-consuming because of the need to collect, interpret, and apply the data, conduct the matches, schedule training sessions with both mentees and mentors, and offer a special orientation session for the mentees' supervisors.

MENTEE OBJECTIVES AND RESOURCES

Coordinators need to ensure that the career and professional learning objectives of the mentees are consistent with and grounded in clearly defined institutional priorities. To accomplish this critical task, coordinators must focus on the pragmatic connections among:

- the *purpose* of the program
- available and accessible *resources*
- the participants' stated *rationale* for pursuing mentoring as a career opportunity

As advocates, coordinators must be prepared to actively shepherd the mentoring enterprise and to take ongoing initiatives to secure the continuing commitment of resources. Organizational support can be demonstrated by such realistic actions as:

- the *quantity and quality* of time and energy allocated by mentors to the program
- the general level of administrative and financial *backup*
- the *seriousness* of the approach toward orientations, follow-up, and training

These factors will have significant implications for overall outcomes. A passive attitude toward securing promised resources could derail progress towards realizing the benefits of a mentoring program.

INCREASED RELIANCE ON RESOURCES

Often, programs are started with reasonably modest goals and a small number of participants, and conducted more on a pilot basis than as a fully operational project. The coordinator, however, must be alert to the intentions of those authorizing the mentoring program.

Sometimes, the initial goal is to expand the scope *as soon as feasible* to include multiple levels of employees in an organization-wide program, such as senior executives, mid-level managers, technical personnel, and administrative support staff. In this case, the coordinator must assess the practical timeframe problem of securing additional personnel and funding, as well as establishing a wider network of cooperation sufficient to accomplish this more ambitious and complex objective. The coordinator should initially assume—unless there is compelling evidence to the contrary—that a *gradual* rather than a swift attempt at expansion will usually prove to be the most prudent and workable decision.

CORRELATION OF SCOPE AND SUPPORT

In considering the most appropriate plan for extending program services, the coordinator must consider the need to build on the existing foundation. By agreeing to quickly undertake the development of a large-scale mentoring project—*especially* with limited resources—the parties involved may be signaling that they do not fully recognize the nurturing, dedication, and general maturation time required for staff and participants to achieve mentoring program goals.

TIME FOR MENTORING SKILLS TO MATURE

The center of a sponsored program is the mentoring relationship, and it should be approached as a sophisticated model of interpersonal learning. Certainly, mentors must demonstrate reasonable proficiency in one-to-one behavioral skills if they are to constructively advise, respectfully counsel, and productively collaborate with their mentees.

In new programs, or in those recently "professionalized," the coordinator can assume that orientation and training will probably be the components most in need of immediate attention. However, it is important to realize that the seminal ideas and insights offered in the early seminars for mentors and mentees will require "maturation" time in order to become an applied and integral part of participants' ongoing mentoring practice.

Realistically, behavioral expertise is acquired incrementally through trial, error, and self-correction. It also relies on a complex set of learning skills, such as genuine self-reflection, nondefensive reactions, and constructive responses to feedback—all of which are essential for productive change and growth.

Typically, the approach to professional development is based on a sequence of steps rather than a single event, and though not always in a logical or ideal order, it often includes the following elements:

♦ formal *training* (introduction to guidelines/standards)

♦ accumulation of personal *experience*

♦ self-assessment/*reflection*

- reliable and relevant *feedback* (solicited from colleagues and experts regarding level of demonstrated proficiency)
- maintenance/*improvement* of skills/effectiveness

OPINIONS VERSUS FEEDBACK

Fortunately, most new mentors share their relevant work and life experience with others, pragmatically assess their actual knowledge and perceived skills, and genuinely participate with integrity in the opportunity to understand how to effectively mentor adult learners in the workplace.

However, coordinators should be alert to claims by those—usually a small number of potentially disruptive persons—who contend that they already possess highly developed abilities to apply their "considerable" interpersonal knowledge. This is particularly noticeable when people imply that their own learning curve is unquestionably centered under a golden halo of almost instant comprehension and competency. It appears as if they are describing an almost magical capacity to transfer relevant learning from the past to the present to the future. Usually, such persons consider that—for them—mentor training is an unnecessary requirement. Sometimes, they may even directly resist the suggestion that their own advanced capabilities could further benefit from involvement in a professionally conducted training program. Because they rely almost exclusively on "self-feedback reports" of their perceived skills rather than on more objective criteria, such persons may *not* be initially receptive to the offer of group training seminars and workshops. Although arrogance is clearly unappealing in mentor candidates, coordinators should still offer them the opportunity to participate, especially in the early workshops. In some cases, such individuals do evolve into capable and conscientious mentor practitioners.

MATCHING MENTORS AND MENTEES

Before mentors and mentees are matched, coordinators need to assess resources and anticipated learning outcomes. Five fundamental questions must be answered by management:

1. What are the primary *goals* of the mentoring program (and is there executive level consensus and support)?

2. Which *groups* of employees should be targeted as participants (and if the program will expand, in what sequence should people be trained)?

3. What criteria and procedures will be used to conduct the match (especially with regard to participant *preferences*)?

4. What assessment instruments and techniques will be used if behavioral/personality/interest *profiles* are the basis of the pairings?

5. What are the *objectives* of the mentees and mentors (and to what extent is there consistency with institutional agendas)?

PRELIMINARY CONCERNS IN MATCHING

After these questions have been answered, coordinators can prepare for the official process of matching. Coordinators should be prepared to directly address the topic of "preferences," which may be raised early in the program. To resolve this specific concern properly, three additional points may need to be addressed *before* matching can occur:

1. Mentor and mentee *expectations* relevant to such matters as commitment, time, resources, staff expertise, and preferences in partners

2. Factors or characteristics (preferences) that constitute legitimate requests because they could have significant influence (such as role model value) on the *outcomes* of the relationship

3. The extent to which participant *preferences* can be accomodated in the selection of mentoring partners

RELEVANCE TO TRAINING

An interesting consideration in matching will be determining the longer term importance of variables such as gender and age on the development of mentoring relationships. Regardless of whether or not this aspect is expressed as a serious concern in the matching stage, participants will still usually need additional explanation about this point, especially if they are unfamiliar with the significance of "profile" as a factor in influencing the evolving mentor–mentee interaction.

During the matching process, the primary emphasis will be on resolving immediate requests for preferences in mentoring partners. However, it is also important for coordinators to mention that this subject will be dealt with as part of the continuing education component of training. Some participants may not have anticipated that preferences would be a topic with implications for mentoring in later seminars, particularly if they had no initial fixed point of view or requests to make related to pairing. Usually, most participants will express a constructive interest in examining this area of potential interpersonal influence, particularly if sensible reasons are offered for including it in the training component of the program.

IDENTIFY MENTORS AND MENTEES

Three fundamental and interrelated questions relevant to the identification of mentees and mentors need to be answered at the beginning of the program:

1. Career development—*Who should be mentees?* This is especially valid if there are options as to which "categories" of employees could form the initial pool of personnel.
2. Staff assessment—*Who would best serve as mentors?*
3. Organizational goals—*What is the purpose* of the mentoring program? This question must be answered so that proper support is provided to ensure the attainment of mission and participant objectives.

There are a variety of factors that could determine how both *who* and *what* are resolved. Certainly, the direction of the mentoring program will depend on the practical allocation of resources—both financial and personnel—to the project.

Once these questions are answered, coordinators can take the necessary steps to establish the foundation on which mentoring relationships can be constructed. From a pragmatic point of view, it is important to launch a *workable* model that can be continuously improved rather than to wait for every program facet to be in place.

As with most complex endeavors, the program can only be developed by the real-world process of *evolving* through its various phases. The pattern of trial, error, and self-correction is clearly applicable to the mentoring model of learning in the modern workplace.

FRONT-LOAD TRAINING

Coordinators also need to be prepared for problems relating to participants' own perceptions of their competency. Many people consider themselves to be qualified in the "human relations" field by virtue of their past success *as managers*. Certainly, individual self-awareness of *earned* professional expertise in human behavior is appropriate. However the tendency of managers to interpret the "official" mentor role as the formulation of, or relatively easy transition from, a prior informal task can be an obstacle to program implementation.

While new mentors may certainly possess considerable interactive skill as managers, they must still be prepared to consider the risk of claiming universal expertise in human behavior. Coordinators cannot assume that positive (self and feedback-based) evaluations of prior interpersonal competency gained *outside* the context of sponsored mentoring are automatically transferable into the mentor–mentee model of learning in the workplace. This is why the initial self-assessment by mentors of their own interpersonal skills and their involvement in continuing training in the behavioral role of mentor are vital aspects of successful programs.

Coordinators should note that a review of the differences and similarities between adult mentoring and other types of one-to-one situations will be included as a topic in the orientation and early training sessions. This point should be introduced without suggesting there are hidden beliefs, such as the assumption that most new staff—regardless of their own self-assessment—will typically lack relevant knowledge and ability as mentors.

What must be stressed is that people new to mentoring usually profit by reflecting on their prior experiences in the workplace. This is particularly the case if the assessment of their interpersonal competencies was obtained primarily without benefit of any substantive training, critiques of actual experiences, or objective feedback. Most new staff will be receptive to the idea that they could benefit from seminars focused on increasing their skills in conducting mentor–mentee relationships.

To deal with the matter of promoting early mentor competency, the coordinator should plan a schedule of orientations and initial training sessions so that all concerned can attend, directly observe, and individually participate in professional development seminars (including role plays).

In explaining this point to those who already place a high value on their own interpersonal proficiency, tact will be necessary. But coordinators must be clear from the beginning that there is a pressing need for all participants to become involved in training designed for direct application to their professional development as mentors and mentees.

The proper training of mentors should rank as a primary obligation. However, in addition to the focus on enhancing mentor expertise, coordinators must also remain alert to adequately developing the other components that constitute the *whole* mentoring project, including:

*   *administrative* coordination, planning, and support
*   *control* over the matching process
*   proper *orientations* and professional *training*
*   built-in *safeguards* to protect the rights of the participants
*   *evaluation* and improvement methods

EXPLAIN COMPLEMENTARY BENEFITS

Ideally, mentoring should be perceived by employees as a coordinated blend of mentee and mentor objectives and organizational goals. As a developmental approach to workplace learning, mentoring should be perceived as an attempt to sponsor educational and training projects, activities, and experiences that offer *reciprocal* benefits—for staff and for the organizational mission.

However, the mentoring concept may not be instantly recognizable as a powerful opportunity to engage in mutually productive workplace interactions. Because of past difficulties, such as the perception of training divisions as too influenced by "fads," some worthwhile programs officially operating under the human resource or employee development label have been unreasonably stereotyped as narrowly focused projects with limited, unworkable, or even hidden agendas.

Although there usually will be a positive response to the proposal to sponsor a mentoring program, the coordinator cannot assume that the idea will be automatically accepted or interpreted by everyone as a *complementary* enterprise with immediate and future productive implications.

Instead, those responsible for planning and developing the program should provide a clear explanation that highlights the *dual* benefits of mentoring for:

- the *participants*—who will have the opportunity and challenge of engaging in the experience of substantive one-to-one learning
- the *organization*—which can gain increased stability, productivity, and/or profits in an increasingly intricate and competitive environment

3. DEVELOP OPERATIONAL GUIDANCE

Many factors must be combined for the mentoring program to offer participants genuine one-to-one experiences, group activities, and special projects that will contribute to their career and educational development.

PROVIDE KEY GUIDELINES

In designing the initial program, the coordinator should provide clear guidelines for such fundamental points as:

- the *length/frequency* of mentor–mentee sessions
- the workplace *projects/activities* relevant for mentoring
- the *content/issues* appropriate for interpersonal dialogue

It is proper for mentors and mentees to count on administrative proficiency and support. However, just as importantly, they must recognize that the success of their mentoring relationship will depend as well on the extent of their individual commitment to create a quality mentoring relationship based on a reasonable quantity of interpersonal experience.

CLARIFY THE QUALITATIVE DIMENSION

Mentoring occurs within and depends on the larger organization. The overall framework of institutional resources will thus contribute to the relevance of the total mentor–mentee experience. It is therefore correct to describe the final learning outcomes as connected to a multifaceted blend of external factors, such as executive interest, staff involvement, and level of funding. However, in explaining the numerous variables that could influence the success of the mentoring initiative, the coordinator should remember to emphasize a major point: the central importance of the *quality* of mentor and mentee participation within the organizational context.

Although a variety of environmental factors will combine to produce the experience referred to as "mentoring," the key to success is found in three critical (internal) factors over which the participants have the most influence:

- ◆ the *mentor's* professional knowledge and competency in one-to-one interactive/dialogue skills
- ◆ the *mentee's* motivation and readiness to engage in collaborative learning
- ◆ the *mutual* seriousness to maintain scheduled sessions, select relevant topics, and pursue meaningful activities

FOCUS ON MENTORING BEHAVIORS

To maximize the learning opportunity, both mentors and mentees must follow the basic program guidelines. However, they must also actively engage in the more difficult mentoring *behaviors* in order to fulfill the learning potential offered by the mentoring relationship. It is often useful for the coordinator to state that one sign or measure of mutual mentor–mentee commitment will be their combined and consistent effort—by words and actions—to meet learning objectives by creatively transforming their increasing knowledge into constructive change.

RELEVANCE OF OVERALL TIMEFRAME

The quality of the mentoring experience will certainly depend on significant factors such as the extent of participant interest and the combined proficiency level of interpersonal skills. However, the *total* amount of time a pair will spend together should also be viewed as a significant factor in anticipating the probable value of their relationship.

From the perspective of *quantity*, or cumulative mentor–mentee contact hours, the salient aspects to consider are:

- the *number* of months in which the mentoring interaction will occur
- the number of *contacts* per week (and month)
- the *hours* available for specific one-to-one meetings
- the time spent in *joint* activities/projects outside of sessions
- the schedule of *combined* mentor/mentee program seminars

DEVELOPMENTAL PROCESS

To fully comprehend the intent of mentoring, the quantitative as well as the qualitative dimension of the interpersonal relationship must be recognized as a critical variable. A major assumption underlying the mentoring model is that it is a time-dependent experiential process, especially in terms of its value for mentees.

The concept of a one-to-one workplace relationship must include a realistic appreciation of *developmental* time. It is essential that the mentoring model be applied with the recognition that a reasonable period must elapse for relevant education to occur.

AMOUNT OF MENTORING INTERACTION

There is no set formula to apply in determining if a *minimum* amount of time is required for one-to-one contact to merit the positive definition intended by the term "meaningful" adult mentoring relationship. However, the *effect* of quantity on the quality of interpersonal involvement should remain a basic indicator of probable goal attainment. As in most complex educational endeavors, there will certainly be a direct connection between the total amount of time participants spend as mentees and the final worth of their one-to-one experience as a source of important career and professional development.

For the purpose of establishing sensible "quantity" of interaction guidelines, two interrelated components should be considered:

- ◆ the *goals of the program* as a sponsored initiative
- ◆ the *objectives of the participants* (especially of mentees)

The mentoring relationship, as a developmental process of learning, should be conducted with the understanding that *maturational time* is a highly significant factor. The unique power of mentoring derives from the strength of the interpersonal involvement at the center of the mentor–mentee relationship. Quantity as well as quality of experience must therefore be included as an important variable if productive outcomes are expected from mentoring programs.

LENGTH OF SESSIONS/FREQUENCY OF CONTACT

For the mentoring model, two hours per month appears to be a workable baseline figure, particularly since the underlying assumption is that mentees will also be directly involved in related activities and projects *outside* of their interpersonal dialogues with mentors.

The specific amount of time spent in the actual one-to-one interactive sessions may vary. For example, mentors and mentees may sometimes decide to meet on the average of once every two weeks for one hour, or for thirty minutes once a week for a particular month. The relevant concern is that *less* than two hours per month would probably create a thin rather than enriched opportunity for the mentoring relationship to mature into a worthwhile workplace learning experience.

It is interesting to note that most managers and employees do not typically spend two hours each month together—one-to-one—for the *express purpose* of focusing on career plans. So, from this perspective, the allocation of two hours per month (or twenty-four hours over twelve months) dedicated to the professional development of mentees can be viewed as a realistic and reasonable amount of time to accomplish the goals appropriate for mentoring.

Generally, regularly scheduled mentor–mentee interaction should be planned for a one-year duration, although programs with highly focused agendas and sufficient allocations of interactive time per month can achieve success within six months. To accelerate the learning curve, the following variation can be used:

1. Compute the *total number* of available session hours.
2. *Front-load* the early part of the program with more hours of contact.
3. Gradually *decrease the number* of sessions per week or month.
4. Establish a reasonably *uniform number* of scheduled one-to-one meetings and activities for the remainder of the program.

Many other options can be explored to serve the needs of particular institutions and participants.

ROLE OF COORDINATOR IN CREATING USEABLE TIME

One of the challenges inherent in the conduct of most programs will be to accomplish mentees' ambitious goals during the time available. Thus the coordinator's managerial skill in handling operational details will be a considerable strength (or weakness).

A valuable contribution the coordinator can make is to *streamline* the management of administrative/procedural details so that mentees and mentors are offered the maximum opportunity to develop as participants in their own interactive dialogues and individualized projects, in planned orientation/training workshops, and in combined group seminars. The coordinator who takes an active role in providing proper encouragement, support, and leadership can serve as a practical advocate for the attainment of solid mentoring relationships.

LIMITS APPLIED TO TOPICS/ISSUES

A fundamental assumption about mentoring is that the topics and issues raised in the one-to-one dialogues will primarily reflect the career and professional interests of mentees. It is important to recognize that a wide range of sensitive subjects can be included under this agenda, such as:

- reviewing the level of sophistication *demonstrated* by mentees as *problem-solvers* to achieve their goals
- assessing mentees' ability to accurately *understand* information and *interpret* experience
- evaluating mentees' capacity to constructively *apply* this knowledge and insight to their own *decisions and actions*
- examining the capacity of mentees to handle *conflict/disappointment/stress maturely*
- probing mentees' ability to *adapt* and constructively respond to rapid *change*

Given this scope, perhaps the most useful way to establish a sense of the proper "limits" or boundaries within which mentors and mentees should interact is to identify the content deemed to be *inadvisable* for mutual examination. Among the most serious of possible concerns for managers and mentors in the contemporary workplace is a mentee's *observed inability to function*—to perform expected responsibilities and tasks while maintaining appropriate behavior. An obvious option in this instance would be the referral of the mentee for specialized assistance; mentors would not be the proper staff to handle such problems.

NEED FOR A POLICY ON REFERRAL

Coordinators should formulate a clear policy on referral. Mentors will need concrete guidance, especially in handling a situation in which an employee/mentee experiences a problem that affects daily performance directly. Such an event would certainly be difficult, both for the person involved and for the organization, and mentors must be particularly vigilant about the *propriety* of decisions that could involve them in continued contact with mentees who are also undergoing significant individual stress and anxiety.

The guidelines should identify performance/behavioral problems that are considered problems because of their occurrence *within* the workplace. Moreover, the policy should specifically address the issue of handling cognitive or emotional difficulties, which if not directly dealt with in a professional manner would actually constitute an *irresponsible* reaction to an employee's distress.

UNWISE INTERVENTIONS/PROPER SUPPORT

Mentors should also be cautioned against attempts to assume the role properly assumed by a responsible counselor or therapist even if the employee remains functional but privately expresses the desire for individual assistance.

In explaining this policy, coordinators might mention that although referral is the proper intervention, this procedure should *not* be interpreted as a signal to maintain distance. In most instances, genuine expressions of support and concern will be both warranted and appreciated.

CORE POINT OF SPECIFIC POLICY

Mentors must fully comprehend that there are usually numerous and often complex reasons underlying personal scenarios that result in serious performance disruptions.

The coordinator must establish and communicate a straightforward policy (at the beginning of the program) to the participants. For example,

> *Mentor–mentee attempts to deal with the causes, consequences, and remedies for problematic behavior should be considered an area of exploration or intervention most suitable for referral to qualified individuals with professional credentials or to specialized agencies.*

HIGHLIGHT REASONS FOR REFERRAL

In informing participants about specific policy guidelines, two concerns should be emphasized regarding the rationale behind *referral:*

◆ an *allocation of time* beyond the scope of planned mentor involvement would generally be required to deal with serious and complicated problems

◆ *Specific expertise* would typically be indicated, especially if the mentee's issues required the assistance of someone whose education, skills, and certification meet the standards in fields collectively referred to as the "helping professions"

Most mentors will recognize that they are not in a position—either through training or access to resources—to deal with therapeutic issues, or to handle related concerns (financial, marriage, children, peer conflict, social) of a specifically *personal* nature. However, it may still be necessary to emphasize that, regardless of how well meaning their motives, mentors would be entering into uncharted terrain if they were to assume individual responsibility for helping other staff confront difficult issues or solve pressing problems. This is particularly the case if the issues create a negative impact on their "quality of life," either as an employee at work, as a member of a family, or as a citizen of the world.

KNOWLEDGE ABOUT EMPLOYEE ASSISTANCE

Mentors should be knowledgeable about the basic employee assistance services available as well as the most appropriate manner in which to suggest such referral.

Many organizations offer help through formal arrangements with a variety of health care providers, and mentors should be familiar with the procedures for referring mentees to staff counseling and employee assistance programs.

Participants should be informed that referral is an option early in the program. The level of information provided to them outside of mentoring may vary from sponsored workshops with detailed explanations and pamphlets to limited and indirect comments garnered through an informal network about the possibility of "counseling" for staff.

CAREFUL PROVISION OF INFORMATION

The coordinator must ascertain the amount and reliability of employee assistance information disseminated throughout the organization. If appropriate as a means of filling in gaps, factual data can be introduced at the orientation sessions in order to inform the participants about employee assistance options— without giving the *incorrect* impression that referral for individual problems is an expected or probable consequence of being in the mentoring program.

The coordinator should neither overstate nor understate the issue—a direct and concise explanation will normally be sufficient to make the point. In addition, if scheduled presentations by staff representatives are regularly conducted about employee development benefits and concerns, interested mentors and mentees can be encouraged to increase their awareness by attending in order to obtain material from other personnel with more expertise (than mentors) in this field.

CHECKLIST OF PROBLEMS INDICATING REFERRAL

Most mentors will be able to recognize when an employee/mentee is experiencing *serious* mental health problems, such as cognitive, emotional, or psychological dysfunction and distress that interfere with performance in the workplace.

The coordinator can use the following list as a guide to identify those types of personal or professional problems for which mentees should be referred for assistance because they are *outside* the proper boundaries of the mentoring program:

- ◆ arriving late, leaving early, erratic attendance, disappearing from office with vague or no explanation
- ◆ missed deadlines, incomplete or inaccurate work

- frequent interpersonal conflict with associates, customers, repeatedly blaming others for errors
- sullen withdrawal from peers, refusal to communicate
- arguments on phone with family or friends
- distraction, difficulty in concentrating, preoccupation with self
- sleeping, dozing at desk, extreme fatigue, lack of motivation.

4. CONDUCT A PROACTIVE PROGRAM

In sorting the priorities necessary for organizing and establishing the mentoring project, the coordinator should be prepared to devote considerable time to four basic and related actions:

- Involve top-level administrators in explaining the overall importance of the mentoring program to the larger organization.
- Clarify why and how mentoring is relevant to the specific professional interests of all prospective participants—mentees and mentors.
- Outline the program development and training plan.
- Propose a timetable of key events.

It is critical that appropriate energy be devoted to building a secure base of management support. The value of *personally* seeking out and requesting advice and assistance should never be underestimated. In this regard, the coordinator should undertake two initiatives to construct a solid foundation for the program:

1. include executives in activities (planning meetings, orientations for staff) that promote their own understanding of the mentoring approach
2. encourage their involvement and investment in the success of the project

To concentrate *only* on immediate and clearly important administrative details— but fail to cultivate the relevant managerial and social network with its underlying potential to generate formal and informal positive influence—will usually prove to be a costly mistake.

ENLIST THE LEADERSHIP

Coordinators, especially of pilot projects, should enlist the *visible* advocacy of senior administrators as part of the campaign to advertise the merits of new programs. The involvement of the executive leadership and managers can add thrust to the momentum of a sponsored initiative.

It is worth noting that not all top-level officials may be aware of the importance of their own *public* endorsement as a vital factor in the successful launch of a mentoring project. Even if they proposed the concept, some executives may believe that their direct assistance has ended with the decision to designate sufficient personnel and resources to start a meaningful program.

Moreover, the idea to initiate a sponsored program may have originated from sources *other* than senior staff. In some cases, mentoring may be suggested by junior personnel and then later approved by upper-level managers who may not be fully aware—unless they are properly informed—that their personal influence could add significant credibility to the coordinator's effort to introduce the project.

A clear message of support by respected staff (in writing and at meetings) can send an important signal of serious senior commitment to the goals of mentoring. Two main points those at the executive level should be encouraged to highlight in their written statements and initial public presentations are:

◆ the particular *benefits* of the new initiative for mentees and mentors
◆ the general *value* of mentoring for the whole organization

FOLLOW-UP TO CREATE EARLY CREDIBILITY

Coordinators must recognize that even though the constructive actions of respected managers may produce the desired "halo effect," the glow may dim quickly if prompt follow-up does not immediately occur after their encouraging words.

While there will usually be individuals who are eager to participate in a newly announced mentoring program, a painfully slow start may enable the usual chorus of skeptics to dampen initial enthusiasm. Lack of immediate follow-through may also be interpreted by interested employees as a lack of commitment to the proposed initiative.

In addition, a disorganized effort may diminish the credibility of the program and thus increase rather than decrease the problem of breaking free of the inertia often faced by such challenging endeavors. It is therefore important that the coordinator accomplish a reasonably quick turnaround time between the advertisement of the program and the first meetings with interested members of the organization.

DEFUSE POSSIBLE CYNICISM

An important early task for the coordinator may be to defuse the possibly cynical perception that the new mentoring program is just another fad eventually destined for the dustbin of failed initiatives.

While the power of verbal advocacy may be sufficient to start a program, even a "blessing" from the highest officials should not be viewed as:

- a message that instantly creates widespread acceptance
- an automatic guarantee of sustained involvement

Today, many employees have already witnessed a repetitive and disquieting event—the loud drum and bugle corps fanfare touting the latest training idea, and then, its gradual and sometimes even rapid diminishment from priority status into a casualty of quiet indifference.

Instead of assuming a defensive posture and apologizing for past disappointments, the coordinator should attempt to energize the workforce at meetings with honest explanations that:

- *emphasize* the overall potential for mentoring to be a constructive initiative for the overall organization
- *clarify* the positive benefits to employees in concrete terms which directly relate to their career/professional development issues

♦   *demonstrate* with examples that the one-to-one method is a widely respected and effective approach for promoting one-to-one workplace learning

5.   COORDINATE WITH MENTEES' SUPERVISORS

The extent to which the supervisory staff should be involved in the mentoring program will usually reflect three important concerns:

1.   Will they be expected to provide *input* into the decisions and plans arrived at between mentors and mentees regarding acceptable learning goals?
2.   Will their *approval* be required to authorize mentees' time away from their primary jobs, or to provide resources to support the mentees' participation in activities?
3.   Will they be directly *supervising* any on-the-job work performed by mentees after mentors have agreed that such projects qualify as mentoring learning objectives?

For example, in some organizations, there are requirements that the supervisor and the employee (not necessarily as a "mentee") agree on an Individual or Professional Development Plan. This document is typically an official guide to courses, workshops, and internships relevant to the knowledge and proficiencies suited to the employee's job series and career advancement. Such plans are often constructed prior to the employee's selection as a mentee, and are not a result of being in a mentoring program. In these instances, the supervisor's input and approval could serve as a factor in shaping the mentee's view of which undertakings are already officially preferred or recognized as a training priority by management.

CONDUCT AN ORIENTATION FOR MENTEES' SUPERVISORS

To deal with the potential issue of defining acceptable mentoring activities, coordinators should promote awareness of the mentoring program assuring all executives, managers, and supervisors in order to influence their willingness to offer positive suggestions and to support mentee growth. The more informed and convinced they are as a group, the more likely the resources of the whole organization will be made available to the participants in the program.

One important way coordinators can generate interest and understanding is to plan a *separate orientation* in the early phase of program development. This session would be especially applicable in cases where supervisors will be expected to contribute time, energy, and resources to the mentoring project.

6.   EVALUATE THE RESULTS

Two basic types of evaluation should be considered for the mentoring program: *formative* and *summative*. It is important to consider the merit of each approach because their combined use can offer information about:

- the present status of the program's operation
- cumulative retrospective data

The purpose of both methods—to provide reliable and valid factual insight into the functioning of mentoring relationships (fulfillment of objectives)—will be covered separately.

FORMATIVE EVALUATION:
FEEDBACK DURING PROGRAM OPERATION

Formative evaluation attempts to determine if mentees are *currently* experiencing benefits from one-to-one developmental learning and to gather mentors' ideas regarding topics (such as planned training) to facilitate that learning.

Such knowledge is important because the results provide *immediate* feedback to the coordinator so that corrective action may be taken as soon as possible. Typically, both mentors and mentees are asked to comment on the extent to which they are:

- engaging in relevant dialogues
- pursuing appropriate projects and activities

- moving at a reasonable rate through learning experiences
- meeting proper objectives for that phase of the program

Because time is limited, coordinators should seek individual feedback in order to ascertain if established goals are being met during the operation of the program. Obviously, problems that are unrecognized and unreported cannot be solved.

Often, *timely* awareness of a particular issue will be a critical factor in determining the final value of a proposed solution. Coordinators' proactive attempt to utilize personnel and resources efficiently can often help to maximize goal attainment.

METHODS OF COLLECTING FORMATIVE INFORMATION

There are three basic approaches for collecting formative information that enable both an adequate assessment of facts and an acceptable response time if an intervention is appropriate:

- group sessions—for public comments or questions
- private discussions—on or off the record
- brief checklists/surveys—for facts and opinions

The coordinator should mention that two of the avenues for sharing such views—follow-up group sessions and private dialogues—offer opportune times for *early* suggestions about any facet of the mentoring program.

In addition, the distribution of brief questionnaires on a regular basis can be used to solicit opinions and viewpoints. These simplified survey instruments usually consist of focused checklists that cover:

- frequency and length of mentoring sessions
- types of issues and topics reviewed
- projects proposed
- activities undertaken

- short sections for personal opinions relevant to any aspect (positive or negative) of the program

EMPHASIS ON SOLUTIONS

At the orientations, the coordinator should announce an "open door" policy and genuine willingness to explore all sides of any problem with mentors and mentees, especially with regard to such matters as personality conflicts or disagreement over policies or procedures.

Because many people under stress reveal a tendency to affix blame and engage in the unproductive activity of searching for "culprits," the coordinator should *directly* state that accusatory behavior is unacceptable.

Participants need to understand that the purpose of both formative and summative surveys is to identify problems in order to formulate workable solutions and responses to those problems. At the earliest opportunity, the coordinator should highlight that improvement rather than mere criticism is the goal of the feedback and data collection effort.

All concerned must undertake sincere commitment to honest and constructive input so that continuing assessment and continuous *improvement* can truly become integral components of the mentoring program.

REASONABLE TURNAROUND TIME

The timeframe between problem identification and proposed solution must be relatively quick to present small issues from becoming larger concerns due to inaction.

As a practitioner of prudent intervention, the coordinator must guard against:

- overreacting to individual assertions regarding problems
- generalizing about the whole enterprise based on a limited sample of participants

Any issue that is raised must be examined in enough depth to clarify its actual significance to mentors or mentees. However, the coordinator must also avoid a snail-like effort in dealing with serious problems. Unexplained, slow, or prolonged administrative response time to participant concerns that have been clearly identified signal an unwillingness (intended or not) to confront and resolve legitimate issues, and thereby detract from the credibility of the program.

VALUE OF FORMATIVE DATA

From the participants' perspective, the data that is collected *while* they are directly involved in the one-to-one experience can provide valuable insight into their current assessment of program success because it will reveal:

- the extent to which *mentees* believe their career development goals are being realized
- the degree to which *mentors* consider that their own professional involvement in the program is contributing to meaningful workplace mentoring experiences

SUMMATIVE DATA: FOLLOWING COMPLETION OF PROGRAM

Typically, the distribution of surveys *following* completion of the program has been viewed as standard practice. Depending on their individual concerns, coordinators can also utilize assessment instruments for the purpose of gathering retrospective information about relevant pragmatic dimensions, with special attention to:

- administrative staff support
- orientation and training seminars
- participant matching
- mentor/mentee interests, skills, and commitment
- assistance with specific problems
- organizational resources

These factors should be considered as important components, which in combination will contribute to the overall success of the mentoring program. They should certainly be included as items for summative evaluation.

COMPREHENSIVE ASSESSMENT

In determining if the mentoring program is fulfilling its purpose, the coordinator should plan to assess both current functioning as well as past operational strength or weakness. By utilizing *both* formative and summative evaluation approaches, the information that is collected can provide immediate feedback at planned checkpoints—and allow for necessary interventions and corrective actions—as well as supply data for future program improvement.

Identifying Participants

◆

1. ESTABLISH INSTITUTIONAL PRIORITIES

A clear vision of organizational priorities is of particular relevance because this will impact the development of the mentoring project directly. Five interrelated points should be considered as highly significant:

- establishing the specific learning *goals* of the program
- allocating *resources* (staff and funds)
- identifying those *personnel* who would probably be the most suitable mentors
- planning the type of *orientations and training* which would best serve participants
- determining the group session *topics* for mentors and mentees

Generally agreed to (stated) priorities will be a worthy contribution to maintaining a workplace environment conducive to one-to-one learning.

In the planning stage, three additional concerns should be clarified regarding the *purpose* of mentoring as a sponsored program:

- the *consistency* of mentoring program goals with the organization's general employee development priorities
- the direct *connection* between the institutional mission and the individual objectives of employees as mentees and professional staff as mentors
- the rationale for the *continued support* of mentoring activities and projects as a training initiative that might be viewed as parallel to other employee learning opportunities

It is important to base decisions on priorities established *early* in the program. The actual influence of initial planning on the later phases of program development can be critical to sustaining genuine momentum. Productive changes necessary to improve daily operations are quite different from disruptive and unproductive changes due to lack of initial clarity.

DEVELOPMENT/EQUITABLE ACCESS TO TRAINING

Ideally, the mentoring program should address and reinforce two related concerns:

- the career development needs of individuals
- the growth and productivity of the organization

However, it is important to recognize that for some employees, the mere mention of training may trigger heated perceptions of managerial favoritism and not-so-hidden agendas rather than be greeted as a legitimate attempt to provide all staff with equal opportunity for development of their competencies. It may therefore still be necessary—even in today's enlightened workplace—to examine the charge that *bias*—whether due to race, gender, age, disability, or any other factor—is operating within some departments. Certainly, *fair* treatment must be ensured.

PREPARE FOR QUESTIONS ABOUT EQUITY

Coordinators should anticipate the possibility of heightened sensitivity to the introduction of one-to-one programs designed to promote career and professional development. If there is a background of past "negative" experience regarding discrimination, that fact alone may cause suspicions to be aroused or displaced onto even the most equitably fashioned mentoring initiative.

If equity is perceived as a pervasive problem (and provokes overt charges of favoritism or prejudice), coordinators should not be surprised if they are *personally* confronted at the initial explanatory or group orientations. Although coordinators should not allow themselves to become surrogate punching bags for those with grievances (even legitimate ones), they must avoid overreacting to implied allegations of insincere motives or bad faith.

Instead, program managers (and senior executives, if present) must attempt to respond calmly to what can sometimes be strong criticism. Often, a useful first response is to acknowledge that the skepticism being expressed is an understandable reaction. It is important to remember that employees who are angry about injustice are not easily satisfied by words, however well intentioned. Usually, only positive action will convince them they are not merely recipients of a condescending stock response.

If openly challenged, coordinators, as mature individuals, should be prepared to patiently, rationally, and assertively focus on two significant points in an effort to resolve issues of bias or discrimination:

- clarifying the *rationale* for establishing the mentoring program
- explaining the *policy* regarding selection/access to this specific training opportunity

Coordinators must remember that employees may have direct questions about the past as well as doubts about the current program. If internal stresses and conflicts are present, the introduction of a mentoring program may be viewed by dissatisfied staff as a continuation of the status quo.

Coordinators who anticipate that equity will surface as an issue should prepare to deal with two fundamental points:

- questions about how employees were selected to attend training/education programs in the past

- questions about how (allegedly) excluded employees will be included in this development activity

In dealing with this problem, it is important that coordinators avoid two unproductive responses, each of which could severely jeopardize the integrity of the mentoring initiative:

- *overreacting* by assuming that all expressed concerns were motivated by misinformed or malcontented persons
- *underreacting* by allowing inappropriately aggressive and relentless verbal assaults to go unanswered

Ideally, the topic of fairness should be be approached in a *proactive* rather than merely a reactive manner. As part of their responsibility, coordinators should directly ascertain (often with the assistance of other appropriate staff) the status of two critical points relevant to equal opportunity:

- the extent to which issues of access to desirable training (and promotion) activities are currently viewed as a problem of inequitable treatment
- the degree such perceptions accurately reflect substantive problems that may actually need to be addressed and resolved

Coordinators can play a significant role by communicating a sensitive and respectful appreciation for the concerns of employees about underlying problems, and thus help to alleviate the misleading impression that they—as management representatives—are unconcerned or oblivious to issues of fair treatment. Mentoring must be concerned with productive change and meaningful opportunity.

ORGANIZATIONAL CULTURE

As a sponsored one-to-one relationship nurtured within a complex organization, the *context* in which mentoring will occur is especially relevant. The merit of the program as an administrative undertaking will initially be determined by the collective view of employees, as well as by the direct perception of those who engage in mentoring relationships.

Certainly, it is both correct and responsible for individuals to question the "legitimacy" of previous employee training programs suspected of inequitable treatment and to challenge institutional inertia toward correcting injustice. However, for participants to prosper, they should be prepared to engage in a *reciprocal good faith effort* without unrealistically expecting the mentoring project to be the magical answer to all serious institutional conflicts.

With this in mind, coordinators should not be expected to inappropriately apologize for honestly attempting to participate in what they interpret as a positive staff development project. Coordinators must be respectful, attentive, and responsive to the concerns of persons with grievances against the organization—but not intimidated.

Moreover, if there is a history of dispute regarding sponsorship and access to training, one beneficial approach to larger institutional problems could be the serious consideration of *expanding* the mentoring pilot project to ensure that it is an inclusive rather than an exclusive program. In this case, it would be important for the coordinator to announce this proposed plan publicly. Also, the earlier this decision is reached, the more likely that initial skeptical reactions can be minimized.

Coordinators must remember that mentoring will operate in the real world of less than perfect environments. It is essential for them to remain optimistic even when confronted with problems that are difficult to resolve. Moreover, they must recognize the importance of their own individual commitment to positive actions, and the value of their own productive energy in conducting ethical and viable programs that offer meaningful opportunities to employees.

2. DETERMINE MENTEE ENTRY ROUTE

There are numerous ways for mentees to enter the mentoring program. However, in most cases, the process follows one of two major approaches: *nonselective* or *selective*. Thus the basic consideration in determining mentee entry route is to decide *what criteria* (if any) will be used to screen candidates in or out of the program.

It should be noted that *some* guidelines will be needed—even if minimal—for all entry routes, because the extent of commitment to both personnel and financial support will impose limits on the number of participants any program can accommodate at one time.

A central point should be to ensure that added administrative complexity and costs are justified with respect to meeting the fundamental goals of the program. There must, of course, be a reasonable correlation between the organizational allocation of resources and the expectation of productive outcomes.

NONSELECTIVE APPROACH

A true nonselective approach would allow *all* interested mentees to be matched to a mentor because there were a corresponding number of available mentors. In addition, there would be sufficient resources to conduct a viable program over the projected timeframe. This scenario, however, is unlikely to occur, and if it did, such an initiative would be a rare event.

More likely, the term "nonselective" is best reserved to portray an approach based on general criteria and limited dependence on procedures. The baseline idea of this approach is that employees *nominate themselves*, and very little, if any, additional paperwork is required.

Of course, a slight variation would be the active encouragement by supervisors, who could initially motivate staff members to request information. Clearly, the decision as to whether the mentoring project should be properly advertised as a nonselective opportunity (or noncompetitive) will primarily depend on organizational goals and resources.

Coordinators should be sure that the terminology used is consistent with the actual practices employed to make decisions regarding how employees enter the program. This can be a sensitive topic (especially in the context of equity concerns), and attention must be paid early in the program development process to clarifying this procedure.

Note that while modifications to improve program operation are usually welcomed, coordinators could create serious credibility problems if repeated changes are the result of criticism and lack of appropriate research and program planning.

SELECTIVE APPROACH

The label "selective" should be used to refer to a program that mandates some or all of the following:

- stated entry and completion criteria
- limited advertisement/notification of availability (not organization-wide)
- application forms
- various levels of recommendations
- program admission interviews
- panels who decide on participant qualifications
- final screening of candidates for admission

In the selective approach, there are many ways to vary or tailor any of the guidelines to the specific requirements of an organization. The more streamlined and efficient the procedural route, however, the more probable that prospective candidates will be comfortable with and attracted to the opportunity to participate as mentees (and mentors).

A PROACTIVE PLAN TO ATTRACT EMPLOYEES

The idea of a proactive effort to interest talented but reserved employees (who may not always view themselves as desirable candidates for mentoring) is a worthwhile endeavor. In actuality, there are always savvy and deserving individuals who are ready to sign up for any activity that appears promising as a career enhancer. But seeking out less assertive persons to ensure that all avenues are internally explored to recognize and encourage ability is a worthwhile organizational goal. Sometimes, the people who could profit most from mentoring are the very ones who, without direct encouragement, would never sign on as mentees. In fact, what such persons often need assistance with is how to be *visible* as a member of a large group.

By making a reasonable commitment to reach out to all potential candidates—not simply by advertising, but also by inquiring through their network of contacts—coordinators can perform a valuable service not only to the employees who would benefit, but also to the sponsoring organization which would be the beneficiary of their contributions to its overall productivity.

STEP THREE

Conducting the Matching Process

◆

1. **PURPOSE OF THE MATCH**

Usually, the main purpose for the mentor–mentee match is to build and increase the various proficiencies required for the mentee's career development. It is assumed that the mentor will be influential in determining the quality and value of the mentoring relationship as a meaningful learning experience for the mentee.

The goal of many mentoring programs is to prepare participants to serve successfully in later managerial or leadership positions in which they will be required to function at a conceptual level of decision making. This is the reason why the emphasis is usually *not* on perfecting specific job-related skills typically monitored by immediate supervisors.

Mentors and mentees need to identify the types of cognitive and affective capabilities best targeted for pragmatic development within the time and resources available to them. Because of their interdependency, participants should be encouraged to view their time together as a *collaborative developmental opportunity* to support quality mentee learning.

2.   THE SUBJECT OF PREFERENCES

Usually, the subject of preferences will be covered in substantive depth in the training seminars, but it will also be relevant in the early sessions in which the matching of participants is the central theme. It is difficult to predict the level of interest and concern participants will have in individual preferences, but coordinators should plan to examine the point.

It is important to place the subject of "preferences" in a meaningful historical, cultural, and business context. A comprehensive approach will enable both mentors and mentees to review their assumptions and beliefs about the implications of preferences such as age or authority for their own mentoring relationship.

Coordinators should indicate that the issue of preferences is worthy of serious consideration because of its assumed—as well as actual—power to influence a mentoring relationship. It should not be introduced as merely an academic exercise or as a mechanical consideration of what personality instrument (there are many available) to select as the basis for a pairing.

Although the mentor as a role model is normally expected to exert a constructive influence on a mentoring relationship, in some programs this particular dimension may assume much more significance—especially with respect to factors such as gender or race. Not surprisingly, when an important reason for sponsoring mentoring *is* the role model value of the mentor, the topic will quite naturally occupy an important place in discussions about its impact on workplace learning.

If the area of individual preferences does not surface or is not viewed as a concern, coordinators still need to alert mentors and mentees to the potential for certain factors to impact (productively or not) on relationships. It is usually necessary to offer a *balanced* assessment regardless of whether or not the participants initially believe these factors can affect their mentoring interaction.

In addition, it is important to realize that even individuals who believe some variables can influence mentor–mentee relationships do not share uniform opinions as to exactly *how* these factors translate into attitudes and behaviors that are advantages or disadvantages in the context of workplace learning. Moreover,

today, differences in traditional pairing can be significant, such as the cc
porary situation in which some mentors are much closer in age to their mer.
perhaps even younger.

PARTICIPANT PREFERENCES AS AN ISSUE

Usually, most participants—both mentors and mentees—will be reasonably
flexible and comfortable about being matched with others who appear to be
"different" by reason of race, gender, age, educational level, status in the organization, or ideas and beliefs.

Some persons, however, may forcefully contend that their preferences are reasonable and should be viewed as understandable (and acceptable) to others.
They may even insist that their choices be honored. If possible, such requests
should be accommodated, not to satisfy an inappropriately aggressive style, but
because there is no compelling (professional) reason to refuse.

Coordinators must also recognize that they may be unable to satisfy some individuals who express strong preferences regarding their "ideal" partners.
Sometimes, this type of behavior may be caused by bias—relying on stereo-
types—which still may surface in a culture of educated persons who claim to
celebrate diversity. Other explanations exist as well, such as:

- a high level of *anxiety* caused by lack of familiarity and involvement with
  others from different backgrounds
- a *belief* that certain factors or characteristics genuinely enhance the qualitative learning dimension of the one-to-one mentoring experience

Coordinators must be careful about overreacting. They must be prepared to
listen and respond with appreciation for those who express responsible but different views. Obviously, expressions of prejudice are never acceptable, and the
proper procedural and legal actions should be used to confront them.

Coordinators may find it helpful to mention at the orientation that the matching process *may* not produce a pairing in which ideal partners are selected who
can satisfy all of the requirements of both parties. Such comments, of course,

must be offered as a factual assessment of resources in order to prepare participants for dealing with this problem if it occurs, but not with the detached demeanor that implies a casual disregard for others' perceptions.

REQUESTS FOR PREFERENCES

Preferences are often based on the following assumption: that a *commonality of background* will be a definite advantage between mentors and mentees because it implies a shared view of the world.

Such viewpoints are usually expressed as the belief that an automatic *harmony* already exists between those with common backgrounds regarding important ideas and interpretations of life and work experiences. The rationale behind requesting a particular similarity is the expectation that the specified characteristic will tap into "natural" affinity and result in genuine understanding and heightened sensitivity, thereby offering more positive interaction and learning. In actuality, while demographic preferences (variables) may influence the quality of mentoring outcomes, they often do so for reasons other than those typically proposed by the participants. When these factors do exert a helpful or unhelpful influence on the interpersonal relationship between mentor and mentee, it is frequently due to the power inherent in a particular factor to increase or decrease opportunities for genuine learning.

There is sufficient evidence to accept the idea that preferences can exert considerable influence on the professional development of some participants in a mentoring program. Coordinators should therefore approach the topic as a relevant practical consideration and not merely as an unnecessary complication of a straightforward agenda.

CLARIFY DIFFICULTIES IN FULFILLING REQUESTS

However, when certain preferences cannot be satisfied, participants may sometimes require additional explanation and assurance that their views have been taken seriously. In such cases, it is often helpful if coordinators briefly describe the particular constraints of their own mentoring initiative, not to apologize, but rather to describe the circumstances of program operation.

New participants should be directly and politely told *why* the task of forming a mentee–mentee relationship may be less than perfectly accomplished. In many instances, they do not realize that unless the mentoring program has unusually large resources of personnel available to serve as mentors and mentees (and even that is no guarantee), coordinators often face substantial pragmatic limits in their ability to meet specific requests for stated characteristics in a partner.

Usually, after the situation is clarified, the majority of mentors and mentees understand and accept the difficulties involved in attempting to form a group (or pool of individuals) that contains enough "diversity" to satisfy everyone's particular preferences.

3.   CONCENTRATE ON OPPORTUNITIES FOR LEARNING

Coordinators should highlight the critical point of the match—mentors and mentee must focus on what they can *gain* from the mentoring experience rather than inappropriately fixate on anticipated "difficulties." Instead of emphasizing dissimilarities (often incorrectly viewed as *incompatibilities*), the participants should be encouraged to focus on adaptation and the productive learning that occurs from exposure to contrasting viewpoints. Coordinators should emphasize that differences based on personality profiles and personal beliefs, for example, should *not* be interpreted as automatic obstacles to learning. Moreover, they should be encouraged to consider the advantages of encountering new opinions and experiences, which may be equally if not more important in preparing them for understanding and dealing with the rapidly changing and diverse world of international business.

It is also important to mention that dependence on a relatively small pool of *available* individuals to serve as mentors and mentees does not mean that participants are thereby forced to accept a pairing situation that will compromise learning and somehow interfere with their educational development.

Coordinators should reinforce the idea that mentoring is a positive chance to learn without inadvertently implying that the current pairing scenario (*constraints* on choosing a partner) is a diluted opportunity for achieving their objectives. In fact, coordinators should plainly state that the preferences or requirements that many people have in advance of pairing may or may not be relevant to the interpersonal dynamics and planned activities required for successful participation in mentoring.

PREFERENCES IN CONTEXT

In a society that encourages *both* pluralism and ethnic/group consciousness and distinctions, coordinators may be faced with assertions that while *similarity* of background is preferable in some learning situations, *difference* is more appropriate in other contexts. Because this is a complex subject, coordinators should attempt to examine this point by focusing on how it relates to the modern workplace, and specifically, how it is connected to the learning goals of mentoring programs.

In applying this topic to the work environment, mentors and mentees could mutually review (in more depth during the later training segment) the extent to which they bring to the mentoring relationship their own opinions about how such factors as age or gender might be a substantive influence on numerous workplace issues, including:

- using *authority* in a positive manner
- handling *delegation* of responsibility issues
- conducting productive *meetings*
- expanding the general base of *life/work experience* with individuals from clearly dissimilar backgrounds

Because of the complexity of this topic, as well as the often strong emotional components that often exist below the surface of general discourse, coordinators should recognize that they may still find it difficult to resolve issues (and disagreements) concerning similarity vs. difference in an entirely satisfactory manner.

CONTINUING WITHOUT A "PREFERRED" PARTNER

At this point in the matching process, participants must decide if their personal and professional concerns (requests) are so critical to their own achievement that they preclude them from being in the program. As has been suggested, coordinators should encourage individuals to reflect on the positive rather than possible negative dimension "differences" pose for the mentoring relationship.

In most instances—*especially* if included as a serious topic in the training seminars—very few of the personality or background preferences initially considered to be essential for the mentor–mentee relationship to be a productive experience will actually turn out to exert the anticipated (negative) influence.

If employees remain in the program, it should be because:

- they view the current mentoring situation as offering sufficient opportunities for workplace learning
- they have decided that their inability to be matched with an "ideal" partner is no longer a primary obstacle, but rather a secondary issue

VALUE OF DIFFERENCE

It also may be useful to emphasize again that contact with "difference" often proves to be more desirable than continuing exposure to "sameness" in offering a *unique opportunity* for significant learning and development. Similarity, for example, between teacher and student is neither a guarantee of educational success nor is it always preferable to the "stretch" or growth that often occurs from direct connection with others who embody a diversity of ideas, viewpoints, and experiences. Coordinators should be prepared, therefore, to question and even challenge the assumption that all meaningful learning must occur between people with noticeably similar backgrounds.

Moreover, the *behavioral competency* of those persons who have assumed the responsibility of mentor, and the parallel commitment and interpersonal skills of employees serving as mentees, should be presented as highly significant factors in determining the degree of successful goal completion in a program.

Coordinators should emphasize that the mentoring model of learning is best approached with the mature perspective that adults must be prepared to adapt to and compensate for less than perfect conditions. If they share or adopt this constructive attitude, they will be better prepared to work at creating collaborative one-to-one workplace relationships that have relevance for their career and professional development.

STEP FOUR

Orientation and Training

$\blacklozenge$

1. DEVELOP MENTORING SKILLS

The mentoring program involves both orientations and continuing training to promote professional development. In most cases, the approach to increasing participants' mentoring knowledge and behavioral skills will be based on a pattern of:

- general explanations in the early meetings
- seminars to expand on ideas relevant to theory and practice after the introductory foundation is in place
- experiential learning through role plays and group feedback (certainly for mentors, and also mentees, if possible)
- follow-up sessions (at any point) to review topics such as progress in one-to-one learning, relational issues, requests for more detailed knowledge, and status of activities/projects

Ideally, it is preferable to "tailor" the material to fit participants' backgrounds. However, it may be difficult to accurately determine the prior qualifications of staff interested in the mentor role, or to ascertain with any certainty the previous history of employees about to become mentees, especially for a pilot project.

Of course, one possible method for collecting useful preliminary data may be the inclusion of brief questions on the form used to survey personnel who are interested in the mentoring program. Also, staff may request a history of employees' previous involvement with mentoring when they inquire about the project.

2. SUGGESTIONS FOR TRAINING SEMINARS

Seminars are a useful forum in which the participants can interact in a group setting to share their own ideas and experiences, as well as be exposed to new information and techniques relevant to increasing the quality of the mentoring experience. The following six guiding principles may help mentors and mentees remain focused on the essential aims of training in mentoring:

- Obtaining the knowledge and competencies necessary to meet their behavioral *responsibilities* as mentors and mentees in a sponsored program (in seminars and feedback sessions)
- Assessing their own specific interpersonal *skills* relevant to mentoring and identifying their own strengths and weaknesses as participants in achieving the goals of mentoring
- Recognizing the possible impact of variables such as age, gender, race/ethnicity, authority (and philosophy of life/work, personality) on the *dynamics* of mentoring relationships
- Exploring their own current cognitive and affective *strategies* as adult problem solvers in the workplace
- Exploring the value as well as the problems associated with their own *mentoring history* (or similar experiences, if applicable) in past situations
- Considering the possible style of *collaborative relationship* that appears feasible based on preliminary (and ongoing) views of their own and their partners' *"profiles"*

COMMUNICATE POSITIVE ATTITUDES

Even in the absence of substantive facts about the participants, if coordinators develop a structured but flexible approach, they can design valuable introductory sessions as well as establish the direction of the training and follow-up seminars.

In the initial meetings, coordinators must be particularly attentive to communicating positive attitudes that translate into productive environments for psychological and intellectual learning. This responsibility, however, is not intended to suggest that coordinators must feel compelled to present themselves as continuously cheerful paragons of behavioral equanimity. In actuality, coordinators may also need to engage in "confrontation" (pointing out discrepancies) with participants if it is justified as a viable learning option. Although this approach involves the same risk as other forms of assertive behavior, confrontation may be productive if the coordinator's current response (continuous nurturing) to problems is interpreted as a message of approval by mentors and mentees, and thus serves to reinforce their negative behaviors.

As a constructive and even inspirational motivator, the coordinator can serve as a role model who exerts a beneficial influence on all of the participants. Certainly, an *optimistic* rather than a pessimistic attitude should be viewed as a significant contribution because it is consistent with the goals of an employee development program based on the expectation of success.

Coordinators should properly view themselves as *preceptors* of new mentors, and thus be prepared to demonstrate by their own mentoring skills the approachable, open, receptive, and concerned model of behaviors proposed as the prototype of the effective mentor. In general, at orientations the coordinators should plan to:

- offer concise and precise *explanations*
- respond nondefensively to basic *questions*
- gather relevant *feedback* from the participants regarding the status of their own backgrounds (for planning further workshops)
- solicit *suggestions* related to the needs and issues as perceived by new mentors and mentees

CLARIFY BASIC CONCERNS

Coordinators can make reasonable assumptions about the knowledge and skills most participants will (or should) be interested in acquiring. It is important that an organized agenda of subjects is presented so that the participants recognize that knowledgeable staff are conducting the training project. Streamlined, coherent, and concrete explanations with relevant examples are an especially desirable approach because they help to focus the prepared content (as well as the questions and answers) on topics related to the critical beginning phase of mentoring.

In the early training sessions, the following six fundamental areas of information should satisfy most participants' basic learning needs:

◆ the behavioral *profiles* required for maximizing the unique interpersonal potential within the mentoring relationship (which includes the subject of "preferences" as an influence)

◆ the specific *responsibilities* of the mentors and mentees in a workplace environment

◆ the guidance essential to plan a meaningful learning experience throughout the established *timeframe*

◆ the knowledge necessary to understand and productively respond to the evolving *phases* of the experience

◆ the direct *connections* between the dialogue/activities of mentoring and the individual career development and progress of mentees

◆ the importance of *scheduled one-to-one sessions*, as well as tangible projects suitable for promoting selected mentee professional competencies and goal attainment

EMPHASIZE CORE POINTS OF TRAINING

There is a considerable amount of detailed information available regarding the one-to-one model. It is useful to announce that the orientation and training plan will involve seminars focused on acquiring knowledge about mentoring, clarifying key issues, and engaging in group activities and experiential learning—primarily role simulations.

In selecting introductory material, coordinators should prepare an overall approach that highlights six core points:

- the fundamental *principles* of mentoring theory and practice relevant to adult learning
- the *interpersonal behaviors* most applicable to the workplace by mentors and mentees
- the rationale underlying the *matching* process
- the objectives of *training* and follow-up for participants
- the specific work-related *backgrounds* of the participants as a reference point for the experience of mentoring
- the *culture* of the sponsoring institution, especially with reference to past and current attitudes regarding employee development projects

ORIENTATION AND TRAINING SCHEDULE

Orientations should occur as one or two meetings devoted to introductory and overview material. In most cases, mentors and mentees should attend *separate* programs, especially if sensitive issues and concerns are expected to be raised.

A *combined* orientation session for both mentors and mentees could be productive, especially if arranged to introduce the new pairs and thereby jump-start the relationship. This can be an important opportunity to formally connect the participants, not only as partners, but also as members of a collective enterprise who share a common bond of purpose and commitment. In addition, mutual orientation meetings can be beneficial for examining and clarifying more subtle points, particularly those areas capable of interpretation, such as:

- program goals/participant objectives
- confidentiality rationale
- reference policy
- referral procedures
- content/issues appropriate for dialogues
- topics suitable for projects

- supervisor as influence on mentee
- personality "clash"

In addition to the value of well-conducted orientations, coordinators should consider the training component to be a critical influence on the *qualitative impact* of mentoring program outcomes. In many instances, the weakest components of mentoring programs were found to be caused by inadequate/insufficient attention to mentor training, as well as lack of proper introductory sessions for mentees.

THE NEED FOR CONTINUING TRAINING

The naive belief that most individuals already "naturally" possess all of the behavioral skills required for successful application of the mentoring model has fortunately been replaced by a more realistic assumption. There is a clear trend in the direction of establishing *formalized* continuing training for mentors and mentees and away from past reliance on offering a few rather informal group get togethers and then actually claiming that this constituted legitimate mentoring training. The more proactive approach is primarily due to the growing recognition that training in the theory and practice of "mentoring" has proven to be an essential factor in helping participants to develop mature one-to-one relationships in a relatively compressed timeframe.

The contemporary idea is that a more structured and active approach to training will assist in establishing a baseline of mentor–mentee interpersonal effectiveness. Generally, this involves seminars based on information relevant to the objectives of mentoring, as well as workshops focused on practice sessions aimed at increasing one-to-one proficiencies. Today, many coordinators provide a solid foundation of knowledge and participative experiences directly relevant to increasing the interactive competencies essential for effective mentoring.

In addition, special orientations are now being offered to mentees' supervisors to acquaint them with the goals of mentoring, to alert them to the possible issues that might arise, and to review and suggest specific ways in which they can be supportive of the workplace learning pursued by employees/mentees.

Depending on the resources available (the frequency and content of the continuing training sessions may vary), coordinators should at least attempt to announce a schedule of baseline learning activities. A substantive program for mentors could consist of:

- seminars on different topics (with invited speakers)
- workshops focused on role plays and feedback
- videotaping of practice and small-group critiques
- periodic follow-up activities to share experiences, review program support, recommend specific projects, and assess the status of mentor–mentee relationships

3. CONDUCT A SPECIAL ORIENTATION FOR SUPERVISORS

At the orientation for supervisors, the coordinator can resolve basic problems, answer concerns, and solicit ideas and suggestions. This is an important meeting because a healthy *network* of supervisory understanding and support will contribute to the ability of mentees to continue performing as conscientious employees in their daily jobs while also:

- fulfilling their commitment to maintain scheduled one-to-one contact with mentors
- accomplishing workplace projects approved as specific contributions to achieving mentee learning objectives
- attending scheduled on-and off-site meetings and conferences related to mentee development (for the value of direct experience as well as to analyze the theory of group dynamics *and* the specific application to their workplace)

In addition to explaining the goals and guidelines of mentoring, coordinators should anticipate that they will be asked to clarify a significant concern: How the the current job responsibilities of their employees are *different* from their work as mentees in pursuit of learning objectives considered to be relevant to and appropriate for mentoring.

The answer should be considered neither self-explanatory nor crystal clear. A request for clarification about the topics, workshops, projects, meetings, and experiences that specifically constitute *mentoring content* should be expected, especially since a complete explanation will involve a complex blend of individual perceptions, situational factors, and program agendas.

Of course, the "answer" will usually be clear to those persons for whom mentoring will now be *grafted* onto an already established core curriculum of courses and job rotational assignments connected to a Leadership or Management Development Program. Typically, such training initiatives have evolved into a formal and often highly structured sequence of courses, seminars, internships, projects, and rotations. In these instances, the mentoring approach can usually be smoothly integrated into the existing employee development model of learning.

However, those who are involved in a new mentoring initiative, or are unfamiliar with the practice of one-to-one learning in the workplace, will not possess the same reference points as persons with prior experience. Coordinators should be prepared to offer specific examples to explain the variety of components that mentors and mentees could *collaboratively* include in a learning plan, such as:

- clarification of career goals and paths
- review of requirements, proficiencies, and credentials
- discussion of selected readings, work-related research
- referral through the professional network
- professional development projects
- recommended workshops, seminars, courses, and conferences
- analysis of interpersonal and group dynamics
- feedback about the status of current competencies
- assessments of and challenges to ideas and beliefs
- critiques of career/professional progress
- reflections on personal values, job satisfaction, and career choices

EXPLAIN THE ROLE OF MENTOR

Another matter that will often require explanation is the basic definition and role of the mentor in the workplace. In presenting this portrait, it is important that coordinators emphasize the central relevance of mentors as influences in promoting and advancing the mentoring relationship.

Supervisors need to fully comprehend the commitment of their colleagues who have accepted the responsibility of mentorship, and to view them with respectful appreciation rather than as competitive members of what could be perceived as a triangle of conflicting work-related possibilities.

It is critical that supervisors understand the specific requirements of one-to-one learning, and in particular, recognize that mentees will need to actively participate in activities and projects in which mentors serve two main functions:

* as an *internal* dialogue partner who can offer relevant guidance, interpretations of events, and specific feedback during the scheduled one-to-one sessions between mentors and mentees
* as a source who offers constructive critiques from the vantage point of personal experience, professional knowledge, and present organizational attitudes and views—with a focus on reviewing the special projects conducted *external* to their own face-to-face mentoring meetings

REVIEW PROBLEMS DUE TO SUPERVISORY PARTICIPATION

The supervisor, employee/mentee, and mentor may sometimes *all* need to agree on what constitutes relevant mentoring-specific learning. After this decision is reached, the supervisor may continue to be involved in monitoring the performance of the on-the-job duties pursued by the mentee.

Although this arrangement can be workable and productive, two problems might occur:

* *overlap* of supervisor and mentor influence/authority if both persons are directly involved in the mentee's projects

- *conflict* between assigned employee job responsibilities and mentee learning activities that result from participation in the program

The supervisor, mentor, and mentee should therefore be sure they all anticipate, clarify, and resolve any substantive differences of opinion regarding their collaborative involvement in projects designated as fulfilling mentoring objectives.

Generally, most supervisors will be supportive of their employees' decisions to participate as mentees in the program. However, it would be unrealistic to assume that *all* supervisors will automatically realize the intrinsic value of mentoring and instantly offer their cooperation. It is also unlikely that they will be universally encouraged to become advocates for the program by other managers who recognize the specific attributes and benefits of the mentor–mentee relationship.

ANTICIPATE SUPERVISORS' WORK-RELATED CONCERNS

Moreover, some supervisors may be less than enthusiastic about the mentoring project if it:

- impacts on their department's *performance/productivity*
- requires adjustments in the *responsibilities or scheduling* of other personnel
- conflicts with their own view of the particular *training plan* (IDP) they believe their employees should pursue to enhance daily tasks

However, rather than overreacting and interpreting reluctant or skeptical reactions as signals of blatant self-interest, coordinators should ascertain if this apprehension is due to other reasons. For example, this response could be the result of a situation in which supervisors were being "encouraged" to look favorably on mentoring while *simultaneously* being expected to maintain the exact same level and quality of employee (mentee) job performance.

The coordinator must recognize the necessity of reaching out and dealing with the concerns of all staff, *especially* those senior managers who are responsible for the daily contribution of employees (mentees) working at mid-level management as well as in nonmanagerial positions.

RECOGNIZE AND DEAL WITH OLD PATTERNS OF CONTROL

One positive trend in the modern workplace has been the increasing delegation of significant responsibility downward in the administrative hierarchy. However, this should not lead to incorrect generalizing about the scope of the evolving redefinition of manager–employee relations, especially regarding the important issue of authorized versus self-approved official training.

The primary issue is not whether management is still required to review and sign off on requests for training; rather, the central point is the *extent of control* exerted by management over the specific preferences and decisions of employees regarding their own professional development.

It is likely that many with managerial authority will not only properly delegate professional workplace responsibility based on sensible policies and procedures, but that they will also demonstrate well-earned confidence in their staff to make intelligent decisions about their career development. However, it is just as likely that many supervisors do *not* fit this idealized description, regardless of their level of administrative responsibility—whether they are front-line supervisors or senior executives. In these cases, employees in the "subordinate" category could still be faced with having work "micro" assigned or delegated to them because of entrenched attitudes about *all* dimensions of the workplace.

The practical result of such a situation would mean that not all staff interested in becoming mentees are treated as autonomous individuals who make their own choices about undertaking important tasks, especially those projects that have high visibility. Not surprisingly, this older pattern of hierarchical dominance and control may be transferred to other areas of the workplace, *including* employee training and development.

Given such a scenario, it is reasonable to assume that many employees/mentees (if viewed as "subordinates" even at mid-level) may still be dependent on their manager's approval to be considered eligible to attend or participate in any workplace training, whether courses, workshops, internships, conferences, *or* mentoring.

With this in mind, coordinators should be alert to the possibility that even relatively high level employees (who are *also* mentees) may be supervised and evaluated by executives who may or may not support their participation in the program.

Although coordinators should anticipate a reasonable and supportive response to the mentoring project, they should be careful about wearing rose-colored glasses to initial sessions with management. The attitude of individual supervisors will reflect, and in some cases, may depend on the willingness of their *own* managers' to support mentee learning activities. Of course, the collective institutional assessment of mentoring as a workplace education program with real merit (or without) will also impact management's perception.

4. ASSESS THE IMPACT OF BACKGROUND: ATTITUDES/BEHAVIORS

The effect of participants' background involves a complex interplay of personal, social, and cultural forces. A productive response to background factors as *influences* (referred to as "preferences" in the section on matching) on one-to-one interaction will require an awareness of two important and related points. Each must be addressed as a serious task:

- the need to counter the *destructive impact* of stereotyping as a block to creating honest interpersonal relationships
- the need to recognize the *constructive value* of similar as well as dissimilar backgrounds in promoting learning

There will be, for example, both productive and unproductive attributes associated with factors such as age, gender, and race. Although there is the possibility that some individuals will be in denial regarding this issue, coordinators must be careful not to allow discussions in training sessions to degenerate into an obsession with either the limiting or the enhancing aspects of these factors.

Sometimes, participants may overemphasize their own agendas for pairing, and even display resistance in considering other points of view. In some instances, the disclosure of painful and unjust experiences caused by various types of prejudice can also result in heated exchanges at meetings.

DEAL WITH NEGATIVE PAST EXPERIENCE

In considering participant "preferences" as a topic in the early phase of the matching process, coordinators need to be both knowledgeable and diplomatic in responding to a variety of opinions.

Coordinators may consider proposing, as a useful baseline, that there is nothing intrinsically inappropriate or misguided about the idea of individuals expressing their honest "preferences" in mentoring partners so long as prejudice is not the source of the request. Sometimes, it can be as straightforward as preferring a calm rather than a "hyper" personality to interact with for a relatively lengthy and intense timeframe.

However, there have been serious acts of discrimination caused by any number of possible "differences"—from race to weight to religion to physical disability. The topic therefore can trigger quick and suspicious responses because there is often evidence of real bias.

Moreover, if the participants genuinely explore this topic, they may express emotions that reveal just how hard it has been (or still is) to resolve and move beyond painful personal or work-related past incidents. Clearly, honest dialogue must be the cornerstone of such sensitive and honest shared history.

However, for these group sessions to be valuable as contributions to workplace learning, participants must follow the essential guideline of engaging in *respectful* expression and dialogue with their colleagues. The mistaken belief that "brutal" honesty (often in the form of angry verbal attacks and hostile accusations) will be acceptable must be confronted as a completely unacceptable form of discourse in a training segment.

Also, the issues associated with discrimination (of any kind) should be properly viewed as gradually but not necessarily fully resolvable within the time available in a mentoring program. A reasonable short-term goal would be to consider mentoring as one component in helping individuals with a history of negative interactions to reconcile their negative past with the expectation of a positive future.

REMAIN OBJECTIVE AS COORDINATOR

Most people recognize the value of objectivity in facilitating certain types of learning. However, it is important to remember that intellectual awareness will not guarantee behavioral serenity, especially when mentors or mentees share the details of disturbing past events. Moreover, coordinators should be especially vigilant about assuming that they (or others) will automatically interpret reported events as personally "nonthreatening." There is always the temptation to defend ourselves and to superimpose our own experience on others.

It is therefore essential for those conducting such meetings to literally pause and to consciously focus on the objective aim of the interaction, which is understanding events from the vantage point of the person who is describing "what it was like for me." Also, it is necessary to avoid a rush to judgment and the forceful expression of fixed opinions, such as suggesting that an individual's particular responses are typically explained by the usual causes, such as overreaction or oversensitivity.

In addition, coordinators should remain alert to the possibility of their own counterproductive responses in which they:

- quickly substitute what they believe the correct intellectual or psychological or emotional reaction should have been at the time
- immediately reinterpret the event by providing "enlightenment" based on their own life or work experience (as a model of the mature response)

Certainly, accounts of difficult past events need to be reviewed and fully understood. However, what will clearly *not* be beneficial are patronizing suggestions or assertions that it could not have happened that way, must be an unfortunate misunderstanding, or puzzlement as to why it is being reported as a traumatic event.

MAINTAIN BALANCED ATTITUDE

The most suitable approach for coordinators is one that reveals a balanced attitude—ideally, a blend of behaviors that demonstrate an ability to display:

◆ a *sensitive* appreciation of the individual differences participants bring to problem solving (analyzing data, reviewing options, taking actions)

◆ a *practical* assessment of productive and unproductive mentor–mentee strategies with respect to reaching the objectives of mentoring

◆ a *constructive* interpersonal style of communicating with participants with regard to commenting on problems and offering ideas for improvement

With regard to experience as a collective reference point, coordinators should exhibit a positive "lessons learned" approach—applied with respect and empathy. This attitude will create a more receptive educational atmosphere, suggest a more positive view of the world, and offer an excellent opportunity to demonstrate (model) examples of skillful interpersonal dialogue. For participants, the benefit gained from reflecting on the past will be the extent to which they can creatively *apply* such learning to similar events in the present and future.

VALUE OF INSIGHT ON BACKGROUNDS FOR PARTICIPANTS

In addressing this issue, coordinators should consider the possible ways in which specific variables such as age and gender may hinder or disrupt as well as advance and enrich workplace opportunities for learning. There often can be a mixed rather than a uniform response.

In introducing this topic, it is important that mentors and mentees understand that problems attributed to "differences" are frequently caused, not by conscious decisions fueled by ignoble motives, but rather by the power of *unexamined* beliefs to inadvertently limit or disrupt the potential for interpersonal learning in the workplace. This can be an important distinction.

When individuals interpret the ideas or actions of others as being motivated by bias or prejudice, the anger that flares up usually burns much hotter if blatant injustice and cruelty are suspected, and not the more correctable flaw of naive or simplistic thinking. Such deep-rooted problems present a challenge to all concerned when they attempt to resolve issues in a meaningful personal and interpersonal manner. A strength of mentoring can be the opportunity to provide all participants with insight that will allow them to cope with, defuse, and effectively handle those factors that exert undesirable behavioral interference due to stereotyping.

It is important for coordinators to note at the training sessions that it is typically the *lack* of complete awareness or full understanding of interpersonal barriers that interferes with collaborative one-to-one interaction, and thereby *compounds* the negative impact of the original problem. In a way, this issue is similar to the oft repeated phrase: "It's what you don't know that hurts you." Certainly, mentors and mentees are unlikely to cope with or resolve communication obstacles if they do not view them as an important element of their own world.

5. EXPLORE IMPLICATIONS OF PREFERENCES FOR RELATIONSHIPS

The impact of similar and different cumulative experiences should be addressed seriously. There have been major changes in ideas, beliefs, and attitudes related to the workplace in the past twenty-five years of rapid and profound change.

In reviewing this information, coordinators must emphasize that this approach should be considered as a broad framework for examining the cultural foundation underlying complex interpersonal behavioral actions and reactions. Two essential points should be highlighted:

- the holistic concept of the individual is a complicated amalgam of multiple influences
- the discussion of variables (also referred to as "preferences" in the section on matching) is primarily intended to assist in understanding some of the more likely factors that might influence mentor–mentee relationships

From this perspective, the combined concepts of a rapidly changing world and the contemporary relevance of preferences for mentoring relationships can be used to establish a proper baseline for constructive dialogue.

In exploring this material, it is necessary to avoid implying that there is true consensus regarding which items should be on the short list—or how important each will prove to be as an influence on a *particular* one-on-one interpersonal relationship as it evolves over the timeframe of the typical program. The real value of the review is to promote awareness that these factors may contribute to both productive and unproductive consequences, and not to suggest a simplistic or rigid cause-and-effect formula to predict the outcomes of mentoring relationships.

In reality, a combination of factors rather the prevalence of any single factor will usually determine the attitude and behavior of each participant. However, it is also important to recognize that sometimes a single variable, such as age or gender, may serve as a powerful determinant that explains an overall viewpoint because it operates as a controlling principle of belief.

Clearly, the *philosophy of life/work* that mentors rely on to guide their own decisions will be reflected in dialogues with mentees. Today, these views may be located on rather extreme points along the belief continuum, as expressed by:

◆ overt and blunt *skepticism* about the traditional place of values such as loyalty and commitment to the work ethic, as well as reservations about offering social contributions

◆ genuine *enthusiasm* about positive opportunities to be productive as a professional in the workplace as well as to be an involved citizen in the community

In many (not necessarily all) sponsored programs, a valuable objective of mentor–mentee involvement will be the opportunity for fundamental (sometimes unexpressed or unexamined) ideas, perceptions, and assumptions to be explored *openly*. This can be a valuable chance for mentees to critically examine their own internalized beliefs, and to reflect on the rationale for their own decisions and actions within a climate of mature and constructive dialogue.

Another major point raised by concern about matching is the significance of *personality* as a factor in mentoring relationships. In reviewing this facet, coordinators should emphasize the importance of one-to-one mentor–mentee inter-action as an opportunity to learn and practice *adaptive* interpersonal behavior.

Mentoring can be a highly relevant educational experience because it offers a genuine opportunity to practice the art of productive adaptation. Direct expe-rience with this principle of conduct is sometimes a necessary corrective to the expectation that others must assume most of the responsibility for what should be mutual collaborative learning. It is therefore important that attention be paid to examining (in group sessions) the powerful but sometimes misunderstood impact that *normal* differences in personality that can have in determining the cognitive and affective behavioral bent of mentors in their evolving interper-sonal relationships with mentees.

As a reference point for discussion, the most frequently requested or inquired about preferences, as well as some of the classic *assumptions* about their typ-ical positive or negative expression as attitudes/behaviors, are listed in the fol-lowing sections. This material is *not* intended to be used as a source of support for particular viewpoints, but rather as a baseline for questions.

This content will be appropriately applied as a point of departure for dialogue—to reflect on the connection between present attitudes and the cultural situa-tion into which some participants may have been socialized. The primary point is to *identify the relevance for mentoring* of current views held by the partici-pants, not to use the occasion as a forum for criticism.

6. THE IMPORTANCE OF SPECIFIC FACTORS

AUTHORITY

The authority to evaluate, recommend for promotion, or make other impor-tant decisions about employees is of considerable importance in the workplace. However, there is much more at stake than these obvious reasons. The "belt of authority" can also exert a significant influence on the quality of *trust* nec-essary for productive interpersonal and group interactions, a fact that has impor-tant implications for workplace training in general, and for the mentoring model of learning in particular.

Even the most fair-minded and reasonable manager will be perceived as an "authority figure." This is not simply because of often stated (sometimes overemphasized) possible parent–child reactions, but because employees must consider the impact of total honesty with another person when he or she has more power to help or hinder their work situation.

In the workplace, the issue of authority cannot be naively conceptualized as a problem that is avoidable. The central consideration should be whether or not authority is being used *productively* to further constructive decision making, operation, and the attainment of the organizational mission.

Savvy managers practice the art of using the authority conferred on them by recognizing the constraints of institutional reward and punishment power over others. Since the workplace is typically an environment in which power is not equally distributed among the staff, managers must be astute about the psychological implications of their authority, positive as well as negative.

Certainly, a mature perception of the issue would include acceptance of responsibility for the wise application of power by those persons with more of it. But the astute manager will also recognize that the issue of authority in mentor–mentee interaction will usually reflect the normal tension between managers and subordinates.

From this perspective, there will often be more advantages than disadvantages in pairing participants who are *not* in the same hierarchy of authority, because the trust issue is generally neutralized as a friction point. If mentees are matched with mentors who have job-related power over them, or work directly for anyone in the same chain of command, the ability of the mentee to be honest may be compromised.

Also, it is important to realize that sudden self-disclosure about work- or lifestyle-related problems may not always be relevant or proper in a mentoring relationship, because the objective is not merely to ventilate personal dissatisfaction or grievances against superiors, other staff, or the world at large. The often quoted point that "honesty is the best policy" must be placed in the real-world context in which such dialogue is genuinely beneficial because it is an accurate and correct mutual response to an appropriate workplace situation. The concern raised by the topic of trust involves complicated viewpoints and values, and participants are well served if the subject is analyzed as a serious point rather than as a superficial or tangential concern.

GENDER

A variety of opinions may be expressed regarding the importance of gender as a contributing factor to the quality of a mentoring relationship. Certainly, enlightened ideas about gender have profoundly changed the workplace into a more equitable environment in which female employees can pursue professional careers without the overtly limiting constraints of bias—even though complete or genuine equity remains incomplete.

In general, males are often still viewed as more aggressive and competitive, and less dependent on the approval of others, while females are portrayed as less confrontational/nonassertive and more concerned with maintaining good relations with others.

With regard to mentoring, these profiles may translate into interpersonal behaviors in which male mentors demand of other males (mentees) more of a willingness to take risks, are less tolerant about displays of emotional "weakness," and express more interest in reviewing strategies and action plans than in the significance of sharing emotional concerns as a factor in decision making.

By contrast, male mentors are considered to be more understanding of female mentees who express reluctance in taking stressful actions, reveal emotional anxieties, or display psychological discomfort. Also, females are more likely to elicit more sympathy when they indicate that other staff have been verbally overbearing or hostile.

Occasionally, female mentees report surprise at a lack of empathy from some older female mentors, who instead of consoling them as younger (disadvantaged) females fighting for career advancement, respond in a rather stern demeanor with accounts of how they handled similar issues without expecting special consideration based on gender from other female (or male) managers.

Also, some male mentees have indicated that older female mentors are sometimes *too* understanding—that their nurturing style prevents them from confronting them when it would be both helpful and appropriate to be questioned and held accountable for decisions and actions. Too gentle an approach, some males have asserted, has tempted or enabled them to avoid facing difficult problems, when in fact, they would have been best served with a more assertive (not necessarily aggressive) interpersonal approach. Of course, another explanation might be that males in these situations were used to aggressive reactions and were labeling assertive responses as being too sensitive or inappropriately low-keyed.

For the purpose of discussion, the following information summarizes and expands the topic of gender as applied to the workplace. It is critical to remember that the material is intended to serve as a reference point for dialogue. It is *not* offered to suggest that any of the highlighted viewpoints should be used as simplistic answers to resolve difficult questions.

GENDER AND THE MENTORING RELATIONSHIP

A. Male Mentor
Attitude/Behavior toward Mentee:

If Male
- Less empathetic
- Encourage direct action
- Less sympathy with outside responsibilities

If Female
- More empathetic
- Encourage caution
- More sympathy with outside responsibilities

B. Female Mentor
Attitude/Behavior toward Mentee:

If Male
- More accepting of risk involving overt action
- More nurturing if younger and limits "macho" attitude
- More respectful of concern for outside responsibilities (especially if family)

If Female
- Less accepting of risk based on confrontation
- Nurturing but also firm if acts "weak"
- Less tolerant if work reduces ability to care for family

AGE

The age at which individuals entered the workforce can influence their over-all view of ideas and values such as loyalty to an institution, leadership quali-ties, career choices, commitment to the work ethic, view of public service, dedication to family and civic responsibilities, and priority for personal self-development time.

For many, the importance of marriage and family can also be a significant age-related consideration with regard to career choice, workload and hours, and decisions about part- or full-time jobs. Typical discussions, especially in single or two-parent family situations, often include concerns about finding time for children, work, continuing education, and the maintenance of adult relationships.

Issues of responsibilities to both children and aging parents are also of consid-erable importance to increasing numbers of people. The age of entry into the workplace can affect the perception of current as well as anticipated future work and family responsibilities. In addition, the pressure to confront retire-ment and longevity (economic and health) concerns are other points that may be raised.

Because many people will also work longer in their careers, change fields of specialization several times, return to higher education to acquire more formal education, and switch between companies more frequently, somewhat older mentees will be increasingly evident as an expected group of workplace staff.

The previous older–younger pairing predicated on assumed age differentiation will also be modified as it reflects changes in these demographic workplace patterns. Many matches today, however, will still probably be between senior and junior (with age as the criterion) employees, although their ages may now be closer rather than further apart.

This trend, of course, raises the distinct possibility that mentor–mentee rela-tions may edge closer to a *peer* model because of the shift away from reliance on the availability of the older mentor who is assumed wiser by virtue of more experience. One implication for mentoring may be to lessen respect for the mentor as an individual with more legitimate authority or expertise than the mentee.

RACE/ETHNICITY

A central belief with respect to race/ethnicity is that similarity of racial or cultural/religious background will exert a positive influence on the quality of the mentoring relationship. This point is often raised in addressing the role model value of mentors for mentees, especially when terms such as "minorities" are applied to groups that have historically been discriminated against (disadvantaged) by the larger society.

This approach may sometimes be interpreted as disparaging of efforts made by those from different groups who wish to mentor minority participants. However, the core assumption to explore is the assertion that those who have directly lived through the same life events within a minority community will naturally be more empathetic because they share a commonality of baseline experience not shared by nongroup members. This may be a controversial point.

In general, the idea most likely to be proposed by advocates of preferences is that members of the same group will be more attuned or alert to the subtleties of workplace attitudes, and thereby more pragmatically adept at scanning the environment for positive opportunities and negative bias with regard to the career development of their mentees. Moreover, mentors who have succeeded under the less favorable conditions caused by bias also are assumed to be both *role models* of success and special *advocates* who can directly assist mentees to counteract its demoralizing impact on their personal and professional lives.

Demographics are changing with respect to the particular factors of ethnicity and race, and more minorities (and females) are now available to serve as mentors. However, this point can surface as a problem in pairing if participants specifically request mentors on the basis of race and there is not an adequate number of mentors who match these preferences.

Again, this is a complicated issue and there are varying views on the subject. The perceptions can range across a wide spectrum:

- the assertion that a major *priority* for matching should be the pairing of persons with the same profile because of the critical significance of the particular variable
- the idea that the emphasis in pairing should be on promoting *adaptive behavior* (even if preferences could be met) by not assuming the central bond must be based on a single factor (such as race) to develop a meaningful mentoring relationship

Conclusion

This work has focused on providing a step-by-step guide to creating a relevant mentoring relationship in the modern workplace.

In considering the complexity and commitment required to launch and maintain a successful one-to-one model of adult learning, however, coordinators should also remember to occasionally fix their vision on the following points that support the daily tasks required to sustain and improve the program:

- The main reason professionals serve as mentors is the genuine *satisfaction* derived from offering one's knowledge and insight to the next generation.
- The primary motive for mentees is the fortunate opportunity to *benefit* from the guidance of older employees who are willing to share their "lessons learned" with others.

Many individuals in the modern workplace believe in offering valuable assistance to their colleagues (as employees and citizens) who are striving to improve themselves, their organizations, and their society. This realization should be viewed as a morale booster to everyone attempting to fulfil the responsibilities associated with the contemporary mentoring program.

Appendix

◆

MATERIALS RELEVANT TO MENTORING ADULT LEARNERS

The following materials are applicable to the planning, development, and operational stages of a modern workplace mentoring program. Each of the works includes its own instructions and guidance for use by coordinators as well as mentors and mentees.

- ◆ *The Principles of Adult Mentoring Inventory (PAMI)*
- ◆ *The Mentor Critique Form (MCF)*
- ◆ *The Principles of Adult Mentoring Inventory Leader's Guide*
- ◆ *The Manager's Pocket Guide to Mentoring*
- ◆ *The Mentee's Guide to Mentoring*

Available from HRD Press, Inc.
22 Amherst Road,
Amherst, Massachusetts, 01002,
800-822-2801.
www.hrdpress.com